ASSHOLES COME IN ALL COLORS

Everybody Has, Is, and Have Been One

A Book of Poems, Short Stories and Rants
About the Stupidity of Racism!

PIAOTT Publishing LLC. Chicago, IL

ASSHOLES COMES IN A COLORS
LOTUSAIRE DEY

979-8-9892562-9-7
Copyright © 2024

P R E F A C E

Who would have thought that the end of the world would be because of racism? Yes! That is how I just opened this book.

Why did I say that?

Well, I cannot say officially that the world will end because of racism, but it sure seems that way if you look at the overall direction the world is going in.

Let me explain.

When you sit back and think of the conflicts around the world, there seems to be one singular basis for the majority of discourse. That is racism, along with all the other isms.

Racism gets in the way of everything. We cannot take care of the world because of it. Using the color of someone's skin, how they believe, or who they love, to degrade, control, and/or destroy their very existence is, in my book, the true definition of evil. Unfortunately, so many people worldwide are fervent practitioners, which is why this book opened with that statement.

Race Groups: HUMANS are based on shared physical or social qualities and are divided into categories generally considered distinct by society.

Culture: is the social behavior and norms found in human societies. It includes a racial, religious, or social group's customary beliefs, social forms, and material traits. Culture also includes the shared attitudes, values, goals, and practices that characterize an institution or organization.

Systemic Racism: The oppression of a racial group to the advantage of another as perpetuated by inequity within interconnected systems (such as political, economic, and social systems)

Racism: Prejudice, discrimination, or antagonism directed against someone of a different race based on the belief that one's race is superior.

There are many ways people define racism, but for context, I will use Merriam-Webster's version. It states that racism is "A belief that race is a fundamental determinant of human traits and capacities and that racial differences produce an inherent superiority of a particular race."

In my opinion, the Merriam-Webster's definition is saying that first, the color of your skin determines if you are human or not, then after that classification, your skin color determines if you are superior or better than the other "so-called" classified races. Racism sounds laughable when I put it in that context.

However, I am writing this book in 2024, and the fact that that definition still exists is stupid, but it's no laughing matter. Who can truly say that their race is superior, pure or righteous when we are all humans and humans are naturally flawed?

Oh! I forgot that some "Races" must be classified as humans first, according to the definition we just went through.

Sure, I know that there are so many people that believe this race is better than that race or their race is better than all other races, but every race has assholes. Every person on earth has been an asshole at one point. Remember, no one is perfect.

Before going any further, I would like to officially apologize to all religious individuals who may come across this book for what is forthcoming. I know there are those in the world who like to persecute others for what is considered "Offensive" language, but some things need to be said. The Creator gave me the words for this book, so feel free to stop reading if you feel offended and take it up with Elohim.

When this book came to me, I struggled with the title due to fear of judgment from those who choose to take the Lord's job for themselves. But God's affinity to the true nature of the donkey was revealed, which is why the title of this book is necessary.

Biblically, the donkey symbolizes peace, strength, and protection and is often used as a vessel of God's word. Donkeys are affectionate, very strong, and extremely smart, with long memories. Donkeys have a cross on their backs that is said to have been given by God for their loyalty and love for the Lord. A donkey, however, can be obsessed with their poop. They consider it their property and will get angry if you remove it, and we know where poop comes from.

What does it mean to be an asshole?

An asshole is a person that is intentionally annoying, rude, boisterous, discouraging, obnoxious, condescending, egotistical, judgmental, uncaring, mean and obsessed with their own sh*t. An asshole is especially destructive when it is being cloaked under the guise of "Showing love." Assholish actions can escalate a person to becoming a murderer, rapist, warmonger, thief, con artist, etc. Being an asshole to someone can destroy their self-esteem, hopes, dreams, and aspirations. I am sure there is a perfect race out there in the world that does not include these types of individuals, correct?

Now, which race does not possess these people?

Don't worry, I'll wait......

Since the beginning of time, humans have fought each other for superiority, a war never to be won by a single individual. And yet, the wars carry on, and destruction sweeps the earth.

The question is, why?

HUMANS are the only species on earth that fight each other because of the way we look, yet we are to have dominion over the earth. We'd be better off if the zebras ran everything.

The struggle for racial power is an ignoramus, ego-driven thought process because to truly have full control is to get all to submit to one race's commands. That is all 7.87 billion people and counting. So, can anyone truly have power, or is it only power in concept? If you think about it, a person can only gain as much power as you allow.

One way we give life to unchecked power is by a small action many believe is harmless. That is sucking up. So, if you find yourself sucking up to someone, then you are giving them power. I should not have to explain sucking up. But it's constantly fawning over someone without merit to get what you want, even to the point of idolatry. We have all done it, some more than others. Now it is a fact that sucking up to someone can cause you to "move up" the success ladder (Whatever you consider success,) but it is truly an asshole thing to do. Sucking up is a practice that has no racial ethnicity. Yet, it is a main component in helping us sustain our mistrust for each other individually and culturally. It is easier to suck up to someone if they look like you.

If racism, along with all the other isms in the world, didn't exist, then people would come into power on their own merits, and maybe we would have a better functioning world. Contrary to popular belief, most people do not seek power. They want to live happy, peaceful lives. Speaking of isms, what's with all the isms in 2024???? You know, socialism, capitalism, communism... Well, we'll touch on that later.

Only the perfect race can truly say that they are the top race. That means that this race of people is perfect in every way and has the right to rule over all other races. This race does not possess the people mentioned above, i.e., rapists, con artists, liars, etc., or any of the traits an asshole possess.

Also, the purity of a race by blood is pretty much thrown out the window, so it is asinine for anyone to resort to tribalism and assume that they are pure. This mainly applies to countries that possess a broad mixture of different cultures living and interacting with each other. Every race has those individuals that make the whole race look bad in the eyes of the world. So again, how can one race say that they are better than the other?

We've been fighting each other for millions of years, all in the name of trying to dominate one another; why? So that we can have slavery again? Well, we saw how that worked out for the world...

Or is it so that everyone can have the same mind? We also know how that turned out the last time we thought on one accord. We, with a collective arrogance, tried to meet The Creator personally. Sheesh! Just look up Nimrod.

Now, whether you believe this story or not, or regardless of religious belief, let's take the story of Noah. For sh*ts and giggles, let us assume that the story was true. This means that The Creator, in all His Glory, was so mad and disappointed in **HUMANS** that He wiped out everything except one man, his family, and the animals.

What is wrong with **HUMANS**?

The fact is, today, we are literally destroying the planet to gain power and subjugate groups of people into categories and subcategories like cattle or sheep or types of wheat. Categorizing **HUMANS** never made any sense or has never worked out. The world is big enough for everyone to live in harmony, but something within us must control one another. Conquer. This applies to everyone from the nosy asshole of a neighbor to the assholes causing all the war and destruction in the world for the sake of power.

Let's say your goal is to conquer the world.

Then what?

How will it be accomplished?

First, you must declare and prove to all those around you, or better yet, the other six "classified" races, that you and your race are pure and better than all others. And it must be accepted by all. That means that your race, as said before, has no flaws or imperfections and is of pure blood.

Ha Ha Ha! That's a wash!

Second, you must eradicate free will. Even if you think some races are beneath yours, there will always be someone ready to rebel, want freedom, love living the way they want, and would die before following someone else, even someone from their own so-called race.

But let's say that you've conquered.

Then what?

Wouldn't life be boring after that?

Definitions reference.

1 PIECE OF UNFINISHED BUSINESS—SYSTEMIC RACISM - Marie W. Watts, Writer. https://www.mariewatts.com/1-piece-of-unfinished-business-systemic-racism/

TABLE OF CONTENTS

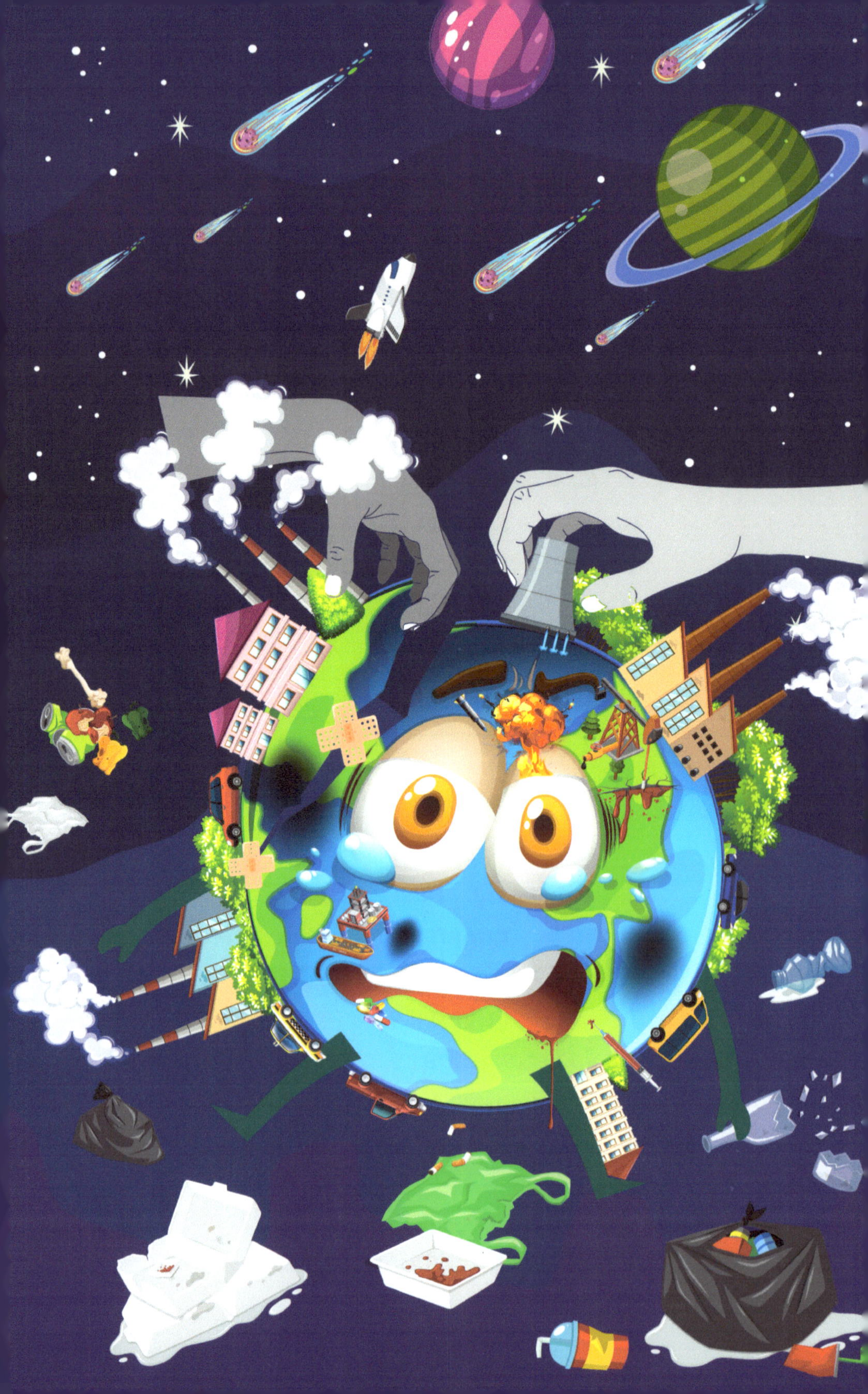

INTRODUCTION

QUESTIONS???
(Talk to me like a four year old.)

Robbing each other for the sake of...
Killing each other for the sake of...
Hating each other for the sake of...
What is it for the sake of society?

Anger for?
Suppression for?
Distrust for?
Sadness for?
What is it for society?

You hate my skin.
I hate that you hate my skin.

Question?

We believe in a higher power right?
Well is it your God or my God teaching hate?
I thought there was only one.

But, we all hate!
Again! Hate each other for?

Awww! Back to the color of my skin.
Because that's the reason right?

Question?

When did Creation give you full authority?
Oh! History dictates it you say.

Question?

Whose story are we talking about?
Your story, my story, or His-story?

And why don't the flowers fight?
Why don't the birds start killing each other
because one can fly further?

I mean really duke it out.

Wow! Maybe. Just maybe...
The birds and the flowers are smarter than HUMANS!

Boom!

Mind-blowing what the animals are doing.
That whole collective living without destroying each other thing.

Who would have thought?
But, we're the higher species.

Oh! Back to the hate.
We hate each other because...?

We love love love war. Correct?

No?

We love love love famine. Right?

No?

Oh, Oh, Oh! I got it!
Maybe we just adore, pestilence, drought, disease, homelessness,
depression, anger, sadness, etc., etc., ...

None of those?

So why do we practice hate?
So why do we practice racism?
Why are we such assholes?

Someone remind me, please.

One of the most idiotic ideas being pushed during the writing of this book is the need for a race war. No one race is pure. No one knows the full truth about humanity. So, to fight so that everyone is the same and one race can have supreme power is equivalent to someone shooting themselves in the foot on purpose.

The saddest part about the state of the world currently is that we are causing our demise because of greed and judgment, two actions humans can easily change through something as simple as choice.

WE are choosing to miss out on the best part of life. Our diversity. WE are choosing our own evaporation, which is simply silly. WE choose not to see beauty in individuality and uniqueness. We are choosing to erase a colorful future.

Racism is destroying us. Wars, division, sorrow, pain, neglect, and destruction of our world are the ending results. Because of racism, we cannot help each other, heal each other, be kind to each other, empathize with each other, or love each other. We've lost our way, and the path to peace is getting more and more buried the more we try to suppress each other and claim superiority because of the color of someone's skin. We're choosing to fall deeper into the isolation of tribalism to preserve the false idea of grandiose absolutism of one race or another.

We should start asking questions like the four year old, because racism is asinine. You cannot take physical possessions with you when you die, and our passions and beliefs should be just that: OURS! But the desire...excuse me, obsession that we have to impose our wills on each other has consumed us. And yet, again, which person can say that their race is perfect without murderers, thieves, rapists, liars, cheaters, swindlers, abusers, psychopaths, and all-around horrible people.

None can say that they are pure because we know that Assholes Come In All Colors.

1 MISSING FAITH

Walking down the streets can be a nightmare these days. There are so many different types of people everywhere now. I really wished they would do something about all these strange people moving into my area!

These thoughts ran through the plainly dressed lady's mind as she walked to the bus stop. "UGH!" She whispered. "There goes one now."

Just ahead was a thin man sitting on the bench a few feet from the bus stop. He had a unique hairstyle and strange clothing. The plainly dressed lady had never seen anyone dress like him before, but as she got closer, she could see that he was dirty. Instantly, she thought that he was homeless, so she became afraid. Her heart began pounding to the beat of her footsteps, and although she was walking fast, it seemed the bus stop was miles away. She was breathing heavily as if she had been running, and sweat started dripping down the back of her neck.

Before the plainly dressed lady knew it, she was standing right next to the thin man with weird hair and strange but dirty clothes. Staring straight ahead, the plainly dressed lady began clutching her purse tightly and side-stepping away from the thin man. Deep down in her spirit, the plainly dressed woman knew that this thin man with this strange hair and crazy yet dirty clothes would rob her for sure.

Where is this bus? She thought. *I'll be glad when it gets here. I know he's going to attack me at any moment.* The bus was taking ages to get there. Longer than usual, according to the plainly dressed lady. And the longer the bus took, the more the plainly dressed lady's mind wandered. The more her mind wandered, the more she became afraid, and yet, the thin man was not paying any attention to her.

I wonder if he's plotting his attack. I bet he does this all the time. I dress plainly so people don't think I have money. I go to worship every week, and I'm a true believer. I bet he doesn't believe like I believe. Look at him. He's thinking of taking my things. I work hard for what I have, so how dare he try to take my money! Doesn't he know that money is everything? But I have Faith, and he cannot take my money. The plainly dressed lady shifted her posture and turned her back slightly to the thin man to hide her now scrunched-up face.

Her wild thinking continued. I should ask him who he worships. I bet it's something evil. Na! That's ok. He'll probably punch me in the face. But look at him. Does he need help? My beliefs say that I should help him, but he will rob me for sure. Plus, doesn't he know I work hard and have bills? I also need to buy this new television that is coming out. I'm tired of the one I have. Come to think of it, I should get a new TV stand to go with it. Or better yet, I'll change my whole living room set. That's what I'll do. So, I can't help this guy because I need my money. I pray he don't want to take it because I need it, and I work hard for this money in my pocket.

Just then, snapping the plainly dressed lady out of her dreamlike state was the thin man with the unique hair and the different yet dirty clothes.

"Hey, lady!" He snapped. "Wake up, the bus is coming."

Startled, the plainly dressed lady squeaked out her mouth, "Oh! Sorry. Thank You."

The sound of the bus completely brought her back to reality as it was pulling up right in front of her. As the doors opened, she looked up at the driver with a sigh of relief, as if he had just rescued her from a maniac.

The bus was fairly quiet because there were only five other riders. The plainly dressed lady began to relax. She was riding to the end of the line and had never seen the thin man before, so she was sure she would be the last to get off the bus. Her mind wandered as she thought of the hair, clothes, and strangeness of the thin man now sitting four rows behind her.

Goodness, she thought. *I am so glad this bus came. I just knew that my time was up because that man just didn't look right. I'm sure that everyone on this bus would agree with me. Anyway, I'm sure he will get off before me, and I will never see him again. I pray that he doesn't hurt anyone. The news said people like that are criminals.*

Laughing to herself, the plainly dressed lady closed her eyes, confident that she was safe.

After twenty minutes, the lady opened her eyes. To her dismay, she was not alone on the bus as she had been on previous rides. There were two other passengers on the bus with her. There was a plainly dressed man, one who looked and dressed much like herself, and the thin man with strange hair and dirty clothing. To herself, she began to panic. Her stop was coming next, and it was the end of the line. She could not ride any further and didn't know what to do. But just then, she thought of the plainly dressed man. She felt safe with him because he looked and dressed like her.

She began to think. *I prayed that the man with the weird hair had gotten off the bus, but he's still here. Well, at least the plainly dressed man is getting off also. Even though I have never seen him before, I'm sure that he has money like me. Look at him. He's probably plainly dressed because he doesn't want anyone to know he has money. That's why I do it. He probably goes to worship like me, too! I go every week, and that's why I have what I have. And that man with the crazy hair wanted to take it. Why is he getting off in my neighborhood? He does not look like he lives in this part of town. He definitely can't afford it. The other guy looks like he belongs, but not the guy with the dirty clothes. Well, we're all getting off this bus together, but the plainly dressed man will definitely help me if that strange guy attacks me.*

The bus came to a stop, and the driver yelled, "End of the line. Everybody off the bus." The plainly dressed lady began gathering her things slowly. She wanted to be the very last person to get off. She definitely wanted to get off behind the thin man, so she moved at a turtle pace. The plainly dressed man was the first to get off, followed closely by the thin man. She noticed the plainly dressed man was bigger and taller than the thin man, making her feel even better. The woman saw that the thin man had walked in front of the bus to cross the street. She was happy because she was going in the other direction. Her house was just around the corner at the end of the block.

As the plainly dressed lady exited the bus, she looked around nervously. She saw the thin man across the street sitting on a bench, waiting for another bus. But she didn't see where the plainly dressed man went because she paid so much attention to the thin man with the different hair. It didn't bother her, however. In her opinion, the plainly dressed man did not look harmful. To her, he looked like a good person.

Walking down this street is again taking forever. But this time, I'm walking away from that man who scared me and was thinking about robbing me. How dare he ride all the way here to my neighborhood. He's probably here to break into someone's house. I should have taken a picture of him. Well, I'll be home soon, then I can lock all my doors and put on the cameras. That way, I can see everything. Let him try to rob me. I can put him in jail where he belongs.

As the lady got close to the corner, she was grabbed, and a hand was put over her mouth. The voice told her not to scream, or it would be the end of her life. She nodded her head in agreement. The voice then told her to turn around but not to say a word, or he would kill her. Again, she nodded her head in agreement. The plainly dressed lady slowly turned around and realized that it was the plainly dressed man. She was shocked. She was so focused on that thin man with the wild hair that she completely forgot about this man, and now he was actually going to kill her.

The plainly dressed man began to aggressively guide her to her house. He told her he had been watching her for a while and knew everything about her. And that what got his attention was her treatment of anyone that didn't look like her. The plainly dressed man whispered in her ear that he knew she wouldn't pay attention if he looked like he belonged and watched her for as long as needed to get her routine. All he had to do was wait for the perfect night.

The plainly dressed lady was terrified. She didn't know what to do or what to think. The only thing she could think of was why she didn't say hello to the thin man with the unique hair and the dirty but eccentric clothes. As they approached the door, the woman began fumbling for her keys. She was trying to stall and think of what to do, but the man grabbed the back of her neck hard and yelled for her to hurry up.

The lady began to shake and cry even harder, saying, "Ok! Ok! I can't find my keys!"

The plainly dressed man and lady were knocked to the ground at that moment. It was the thin man.

He began punching and kicking the plainly dressed man while yelling, "Call the police lady! Call the freakin police!"

Shocked, the plainly dressed woman began dumping out her purse, frantically looking for her phone while watching the fight in front of her. Next thing she knew, the plainly dressed man was knocked out, and the thin man was sitting against her porch rail, bleeding from his hands and breathing heavily.

Hearing the operator over the phone, the plainly dressed lady began urgently telling the operator to hurry and send the police. After getting off the phone, she looked at the man with his different hair and dirty clothes and said, "I'm sorry. Thank you for helping me. I saw your hair and your clothes and knew you were a bad person. I judged you by the way you looked. I could have at least said hello."

The thin man looked at her and said, "It is fine, ma'am. I knew you were thinking bad things about me. I saw it in your face when you first walked up to the bus stop."

The plainly dressed lady was quiet for a second, then asked for his name. The thin man smirked, "My hair and clothes are from my culture, and I am dirty because I was at an event involving dust. You can call me Faith. Which reminds me, where was yours?"

With a confused look on her face, the plainly dressed lady looked down and whispered, "Is there anything I can do to repay you?"

The thin man began to say no, then stopped himself. He then looked at her and said, "As a matter of fact, you can. Don't be an asshole to people that don't look like you in the future. That's all. They may be a great help to you."

She looked at him, smiled, and said, "I think I can accomplish that."

Just then, the police showed up.

PSST!

Consider stopping your judgment of someone based on their appearance or what they may be wearing before it's made. None of us know the circumstances or true heart of an individual. Ask yourself, "Where's my faith?" Because faith and judgment don't mix.

2 ROSE COLORED MIRROR

I am obsessed!

And anyone who looks like me should be, too. All the other colors fail in comparison and should bow down with shame for you being the color of you.

Every other color is repulsive, weird, and don't look very clean. Now, you can hate me for believing this way. I'm sorry; it's how I was raised, so I'm not trying to be mean.

I am only stating the facts. My color is superior to yours. And even though we bleed the same. That reality will not end the wars.

Now I can tell you why the wars won't stop. And a lot of people must die. It's because I idolize the way I look. It's who I am; It's who you want to be. That's the reason why.

When I focus on my race, nothing else matters. People's lives can be destroyed, and hearts can shatter.

When I focus on my color, everyone else takes a back seat. That goes for kindness, caring, humanity, and love for any color I feel is beneath.

Regardless of some of the heinous things that my people do, it doesn't matter because I only know that they're better than you.

This way of thinking may appear to be said in vain. But remember, I told you my color is superior, so no need to complain.

The fact that we are all living beings doesn't matter one bit. And even though we were created in God's image. Everyone must go away. My race is it.

Genocide is against my belief, but it's how it has to be. It really doesn't matter when others are eviscerated if the killer looks like me.

Again, back to the wars, there's another reason why. So many must live in horror, hunger, misery, and millions suffer and die.

I must convince you that what I say is the absolute truth. Because, in reality, I don't really trust what I say.

Do you?

3 FOOD FOR THOUGHT

"I AM," Elohim, The Creator of All Things, Jahova, Alpha and Omega, Mediator, Yeshua, The Messiah, Jesus, Allah...

There are at least 100 different names for God, all of which are sacred. But there is only ONE CREATOR, and He has blessed us with grace, love, and the power of choice. The selection of Him over evil. Sorry, I'm not talking about the Adam and Eve story.

Given the way of the world today, why are so many choosing the evil of racism and hiding it behind the name of God. Elohim is not a destroyer of creation, so to say that this person is unworthy because of the color of their skin is going against God. The lying one is colorblind and will use anyone regardless of color. For hundreds of years, we have been destroying each other because of how we choose to worship the ONE God, or what color we are born as. How sick are we HUMANS to use God as an excuse to hate each other. The "Get rid of them in His name" sentiment is the go-to excuse for the hatred of a racist.

Hitler thought is was God's will to "Sterilize" the Germans of Jewish people and anyone he deemed weak. In the "Divine plan" of natural selection eradication was necessary. Yet the only ones he wanted to eliminate had a certain look.

The Crusades so-called mission was to take the Holy Lands back from the Muslims, or Infadels as they were called. This war is still carrying on today in 2024.

Slavery covered itself in, "God said, obey thy masters," and religious history. But again, the enslaved had a particular look about them and believed differently so they were considered less than HUMAN.

The extremist's goal is to wipe out anyone of different practices of belief in the One God, their culture, and/or the color of their skin. To an extremist, politics, and religion go hand in hand. Whatever the extremists believe is the way the world should be, regardless of what God's plan is for everyone. The belief is so deep that the extremist person or group takes devastating measures to get their point across....bombings, murders, rape, and torture.

So many people have perished under war-cloaked, blood-soaked religion carried by racism. However, God is not of war. **HUMANS** are. He doesn't destroy what He creates. **HUMANS** do. And sadly, it's a choice. Just look at the four brief examples you just read. Each one uses God while going against Him by destroying what is created. Think about it. Even down to the individual racist person who looks at someone's skin, judges them as unfit, unhuman, or disposable, will turn around and blame God by saying it is His will.

How can that be true?

It can't be. Racism is about power and control. Racism is about the ego. Think about it, God and the ego don't mix. You can't have two masters. But we can change this. It takes that gift we all are so fortunate to have. That whole power to choose thing we got.

> **Choose to understand the differences and beauty in creation. We are all created for His pleasure.**
>
> **Understand that our skin varies, but our hearts are the same color.**
>
> **Believe that God is not a respecter of persons because its the Heart He seeks.**
>
> **And know, the heart is where the truth lies, non of us can hide from God.**
>
> **Destroying His creations is against His will.**

4 A BEAUTIFUL DAY

Today is a beautiful day, and the sun is shining bright; the decision to take a walk through the park is an easy one. Even though there was so much anger and violence all around me, I couldn't resist being outside on this beautiful day.

Today is a beautiful day, and the sun is pleasantly warm on my skin, so people's screams are not heard. There is only silence. No gunfire, no cries, no pain. Wow! It's scary. But it's a beautiful day.

With today being a beautiful day and the birds singing their enchanting songs, my brow makes a familiar dent. Confusion strikes my mind. Why CAN I hear the mesmerizing sounds of these creatures? Is it because it's a beautiful day?

Shouldn't I be familiar with the birds and the sun?

But I am not. Why?

Just then, in the distance, I saw a very, very old man sitting on the edge of a large fountain. The fountain was flowing with water that looked like it sparkled. With today being a beautiful day and the sun making the water sparkle, I felt the urge to sit next to the very, very old man. As I got closer to Him, I noticed that He was not a very, very old man but a very, very, very old man with bright white hair in the shape of the sun. He was bent over as if He was in the deepest of thoughts.

The length of his beard tickled me. I remembered this because I chuckled in my throat. His beard connected with His hair and was so long that it touched the ground and swirled in the grass. His skin was an odd color, but I didn't pay that any mind.

As soon as I reached this very, very, very old man, He tried to stand. And even though He had a walking stick as tall as I was, He struggled.

Whew!

I caught Him just before He fell backward.

With today being a beautiful day, the desire to walk with Him came over me like a flash. It was a very easy decision since I didn't hear the violence all around me, and the sun made the water from the fountain sparkle like diamonds. The walk was brief, but I learned so much.

The very, very, very old man told me:

I am sad.

Magnificent are the colors of the rainbow.

Gorgeous are the colors of the flowers.

Superb are the colors of the Animals.

Glorious are the colors of the trees.

And Beautiful is how I made you.

But I am sad.

Beauty is not in the eye of the beholder.

If your eyes only choose to see hate.

And although Beauty is all around you.

It's the choice that so many make.

I am sad.

Different is key to evolution.

You never want just the same.

How would you ever grow?

I never do anything plain.

Angelic are the colors of the skies

Ravishing are the colors of the earth

Dazzling are the colors of the stars.

Stunning are the colors of the universe.

And Beautiful is how I made you.

We were done with our walk. It was a short walk on this beautiful day. We went as far as the bench across the park. He asked that I help Him sit. Of course, I was happy to help as I still heard the bird's melodies and felt the warm sun on my face. I did not hear the anger coming from voices or see the violence all around me. But then it was time for me to leave and go back home.

Walking away seemed painful, as I had never met this man before. But I felt as though I had known Him my whole life. He said so few words, yet what He said was profound. I did not intend to learn on this beautiful day, but I gained so much knowledge unknowingly.

One question I couldn't get out of my mind. Why was the very, very, very old man sad?

I thought and walked and thought and walked.

When I see the colors of birds, trees, animals, and the rainbow, they are beautiful. If that's how I was made, why was He sad?

If the colors of the skies, earth, stars, and universe are beautiful, and that's how I was made, then why was the very, very, very old man sad?

I thought and walked and thought and walked.

Coming to a bench, I sat down. Still thinking, I then remembered.Beauty is in the eye of the beholder, and we choose to behold hate.

The very, very, very old man was gone. I now heard gunfire. I now heard the screams. I heard the violence all around me.

The very, very, very old man was gone. I couldn't hear the delightful songs of the birds. I didn't feel the warmth of the sun on my face, and the fountain no longer sparkled. The man with the white sun-shaped hair was gone.

And all I heard was the anger and sadness from people.

It was then I understood and began to cry.

On this beautiful day.

5 RECTITUDE?

To dishonor my parents is said to be detrimental to my health. The Bible gives at least 20 examples as to why I shouldn't do it. So, with that being said, I believe dishonoring my parents is not good for my well-being.

But! What do you do when your parents are racist? Meaning they hate everybody that's not the same race as they are. They told me I could not play with the neighbor's kids because they were the wrong color, which meant, according to my parents, they were bad. I remember being so confused because the people next door were always really nice to me, but I always listened to my parents. At the time, I figured that parents were always right and they only wanted the best for you.

Growing up, I stayed around people who looked like me. I grew up ok but was never really happy. For some reason, I had a feeling of being incomplete, as if I was missing something or was in some kind of weird bubble. Whenever out in public, I would see people of different races and would want to know about their hair, clothes, or the food that they were eating.......

My parents, especially my dad, always had this thing about "Our bloodline" disappearing. This scared and confused me at the same time. At first, I literally thought our blood was going to vanish, and then my understanding turned into, "But, I thought all blood was the same color. What's the difference if it's mixed?" They never fully explained why they felt this way. Later, I found out it was about the color of the skin.

The way I was raised never stopped my curiosity, but I would get scared remembering what my parents always told me. "People like that are dangerous!" I never forgot their warnings, so no matter how curious I was, my distance was kept. As I got older, I would do anything to stay away from "The Others." That's what I started calling people that didn't look like me.

You know, now that I think about it, fear makes a person do some crazy things. At one point in my life, being mean and nasty to anyone who did not have my skin color was my identity. Hey! I felt like they deserved decent treatment or simple respect. According to my parents, they were not human and had different blood. What was I supposed to do? My parents didn't teach me wrong. Right?

Well, that's what I thought until, one day, I met the best person in the world and fell in love. That person became my best friend and greatest confidant. And the fact that they came from a dissimilar culture and their race was different did not matter. My parents used to say that I could never have anything in common with "The Others," but that turned out to be untrue.

We connected instantly for some reason. Getting to experience the greatest God-given love that I've ever known through this person has caused me to regret some things in my past, like the neighbor's kids. I wish that I was able to play with them. I'm sure it would have been fun. Also, I never asked my parents why I couldn't play with them and what made them so bad. In school, I would see kids who looked like me do some really messed up stuff, but that didn't stop me from treating kids from other races like they were beneath me.

Now that I am grown and have met and fallen in love with someone of a different race, I realize how wrong I was. I'm extremely happy. Sometimes, when in doubt, I wonder if I'm dishonoring my parents or dishonoring the face of God? But then, I remember that God is love, and no matter how we are created on the outside, we are all the same on the inside. And that's what counts to the Creator, as far as I know.

No disrespect, but maybe my parents are mistaken.

The good news is, that is the conclusion my parents came up with; being mistaken. After a while, my parents opened up and got to know my spouse and their culture. It turns out that my spouse became their favorite person. Almost more than me! Go figure.

...................End

Oh! The agony of hatred.

Yes! Hatred! I said it!

Because that's racism. Another word for hatred. I was taught that God is the definition of love! And we were all created with a beating heart. Isn't it funny how the heart is the universal symbol of love and is the same color inside the body?

So what do I do?... ... ...

Myyy parents want me to be with anyone that does not look like me. As long as they do not have the same skin color, they are fine with it. They told me that they wanted to change the color of our bloodline because there's no future if it stays the way it is. This saddens me greatly because I have fallen for someone with the exact same skin color as me...tones included. We're so alike that, at one point, we thought that we were related.... we're not!

Let me tell you a story.

Growing up, my parents had it hard in life. There were many times when I saw my mother crying and my father angry. It didn't seem as if they were mad at each other, but rather some unknown entity that always plagued our home. We weren't poor, but we weren't rich either. There was always this thing that hung over our family like a dark cloud that caused troubles in an otherwise happy home.

Walking down certain streets as a family was scary. To me, people stared at us as if we were a live horror movie. Was it because our skin was different from everybody else? My father would keep me close at all times as if someone was going to snatch me away. We never hung around in public places for too long, and I was always with either my mother or father. To this day, I never understood how that happened because they both worked. Every time my mother cried and my father was angry, someone of a different color was involved. When I was little, we went to a big building with a lot of lights. No one around us looked like us. I didn't understand what was happening, but I remembered my mom crying a lot and my dad being extremely angry. This moment stuck in my head because this was the first time I saw the invisible entity.

We walked into a room, and my father tensed up. After a while and a lot of talking, Mom began to cry. I realized my dad was angry at the person sitting across from us, and the color of their skin was like everyone else who stared when we went anywhere. The more mom cried the more dad yelled. He then looked at my mom and said, "We'll find another way. It'll be ok." She then turned her head and looked at me. There were so many days like the one just described.

It wasn't until I was old enough to date that my parents made themselves clear. They did not want me with someone of the same race. I was so confused about the self-hate. My mom would set me up on dates with people I wasn't attracted to and simply said it was best for me. My father would drill in my head, "Don't date this person, date that person." He would often work hard to discredit the person I liked because they would be of the same race. He would say, "You'll never be happy. You have to marry someone of a different race in order to make it in this world." I never listened.

Guess what? I am happier for it. After a while, my parents began to see how successful and at peace we were. Eventually, they realized that their life experiences weren't the same for everyone, and they both ended up loving my spouse. Imagine the pain of being torn apart because the color of the skin.

RECTITUDE: Noun
- Moral integrity : Righteousness
- The quality or state of being correct in judgment or procedure.

6 CRAYON CITY
The Color of Evil

"Today is a sad day. A horrible day. A day where so many lives have been lost. So many families are torn apart, and so much property has been destroyed. We must mark this day as a day of remembrance so that it shall never happen again."

As I listened to Mayor Purple, I felt a deep pain in my lower gut. It wasn't a physical pain, but emotional. And it hurt bad. I couldn't understand how we got to the point of hating life and each other like this. To see all those pictures on stage with Mayor Purple is heartbreaking. To know that all of them are gone forever is something I'll never get over. The funny thing is, two weeks ago, I would have never thought that I would feel this way. Everything happened so fast. But to see all those faces is a wake-up call. They all are gone. And for what?

Just then, Aldrow felt someone standing by his side, breaking the stream of thoughts he was having. It was Ethel Pope. She was an important person of the Green Clan. Soon after, the very tall and wide Olin Capitis was standing on his other side. Olin Capitis looked orange on the outside but was green on the inside. Aldrow, Ethel Pope, and Olin Capitis began talking.

"What started this stupid color war?" Aldrow asked.

Ethel Pope cried as she looked up at Olin Capitis. With a sad response, she said, "Hatred fed by fear and greed."

Just then, Aldrow said, "It don't seem as important now, does it? Look at this mess!"

Olin Capitis answered, "No! Especially after seeing the end results. Are we that bad that we don't care about life anymore? Two weeks ago, Ethel Pope, I would have said that you were disgusting, behind closed doors of course. And Aldrow, I wasn't even thinking about you. I can't tell you why I have never cared about either of you before today, but I know a big part of this is my fault."

Aldrow looked at Olin Capitis and Ethel Pope and asked, "You see all those faces, don't you? Do it look like either of you care about life? They are gone because of ignorant Color Wars."

Aldrow continued. "Do y'all watch Ruby News?"

Looking shocked, Ethel Pope answered, "Yes! Of course."

Olin Capitis just shook his head yes.

Aldrow then states, "You know they never say anything good about The Green Clan unless you are a specific shade of green, right? They gain more gray tones by pushing negativity and showing certain shades of green in a bad light regularly."

"I don't believe that. I love Ruby News. I watch them faithfully." Ethel Pope said in a stern voice.

"Why do you think so many are afraid of certain shades of the Green Clan? The darker green you are, the scarier you become. Am I right, Ethel Pope?" Aldrow asked.

Turning to Olin Capitis, Aldrow then said, "They don't make your clan look good either. They are always reporting bad stuff about you guys. If I didn't know any better, I would think that all of the Orange Clan were career thieves and thrive on the pain and destruction of others."

Aldrow continued. "The only thing that I'm saying is that we are in this mess mainly because of sources like Ruby News.

Ethel Pope, I know you rely on Ruby News for important information, but you should always remain open-minded and find different sources for the truth before you make a judgement. Because, no offense (Looking at Olin Capitis) the Orange Clan is very sneaky and often use programs like Ruby News to manipulate anyone that will listen."

Aldrow then points around to the horrors surrounding them then continued. "Ruby News only focuses on one color. Gray. As you all do. The funny thing is, gray has no life and, yet it's the most coveted color. So much so that the citizens of Crayon City have destroyed each other. The saddest part about that is the more gray you have, the more murky your color becomes. After a while, everything looks the same."

Aldrow then frowns at Olin Capitis. "Your whole focus was to get as many gray tones as you can. I know it made you feel powerful, but you were killing me and Ethel Pope with all the toxins you were spewing everywhere."

Bending down to pick up a dirty stuffed unicorn he was stepping on, Aldrow sighed. Then handed the toy to Olin Capitis. He saw the blood.

In a low tone, Aldrow looked at the sky and said, "Instead of harboring all the gray tones for yourself and turning your clan into a swamp, you could have used the abundance to make life better for everyone. After all, you are green on the inside. Isn't that right, Olin Capitis?"

Just then, Olin Capitis began to cry, and the color orange began to run down his face. You could see the green underneath.

Putting his hand on his shoulder, Aldrow looks at Olin Capitis and said, "There are only so many things you can color with gray tones. After a while, everything looks the same. As you can see, getting obsessed with the color gray and keeping all the tones for yourself stops everyone from being the shade of green they want to be."

Aldrow continued. "Keeping all the gray tones for yourself also made a lot of the Green Clan angry. The greedier you got, the more separated the Green Clan became, which made them so irate that it has led to this devastating color war. Gray has become the root of all evil. Olin Capitis, you must stop using the Gray Controlism to get what you want."

Olin Capitis looking, at first surprised, then ashamed, lowered his head and asked, "What do you mean Gray Controlism?"

Now smirking, Aldrow scoffed, "You know! Propaganda + Propaganda = Projection. Projection + Projection = Division. Division + Division = War. War = Death = More tones of gray for all on the receiving end. Isn't that why you use Ruby News so much. To spread the propaganda?"

Turning to Ethel Pope, Aldrow sighed, "The Green Clan also got affected by the propaganda. I just wish that you would have thought with your hearts, instead of always listening to Ruby News and turning on each other. That was Olin Capitis's goal."

Sighing again, Aldrow puts his arms around both Elthel Pope and Olin Capitis and states, "Well, we see the end result. But we're not gone, which means we have another chance to fix this for the future. Agreed?"

Looking at each other and then at Aldrow, both Ethel Pope and Olin Capitis gave somber smiles and said at the same time, "Agreed!"

7 THE CHEATING HEART

Dear Conscience;

I know I shouldn't do this to my spouse, but I can't help myself. My love and desires are clearly two different things. I love my spouse, but something about my lover's skin color does something to me. It saddens me sometimes because I know that it has nothing to do with the other person's character. My spouse is great and fulfills my needs, but sometimes, you want something a little different.

At first, I felt really guilty, but I didn't get caught, so I did it again. And again. And again. After a while, it just got easier, and the guilt went to the back of my mind. I don't feel so bad about it now. Why is that, I wonder?

Well, anyway, Conscience, what do I do? Like I said, love and desire are two different things. So the question is, which is more important to me.

When I think about it, loyalty is a portion of love, and desire is mainly made up of the ego. So, I guess I should try to figure out whether I am a loyal person or if my ego is the ruler of my true nature. I need to stop with the infidelity!!

Can my ego handle the devastation that my spouse will go through when they find out? And what about the destruction to the rest of the family? I know they will find out because no matter how slick I think I am, the truth finds its way to the surface. The funny thing is, Conscience, you know what I do is wrong. I figure that's why you're always beating me up, but I never listen to you. Conscience, what shall I do??? I don't want to be the cause of pain, but I want what I want.

You would think that deciding that my love, excuse me, my loyalty would be the obvious easy choice, but still, as I write this letter, I see that I have let my desires... excuse me, my ego direct my life. I have always known that it is okay to love who you love, but we're talking about desire, and that has nothing to do with love. My spouse has all the attributes I need in life, which is something that I love, but my desires lie with people of a different skin color.

I know... it's shallow!

A person's skin should not be a determining factor. I know that Assholes Come In All Colors, but it's just something about being with someone that doesn't look like me. I don't know where this desire comes from. My spouse is perfect. It could be society telling me what is most coveted, with all the commercials and advertising directing my thoughts. Or maybe it's some weird type of self-hate. I really don't know. I should be stronger and think for myself, but again, you want something different sometimes. That want becomes too strong sometimes.

Side note, Conscience...

I wanted to tell you that my family catches the backlash when you beat me up, so take it easy. They don't know why I'm so angry sometimes or why I try to distance myself from them. I don't want to get caught and lose everything.

But....

Regardless of who it hurts...

I want something different...

And even though it's shallow and stupid to risk everything over skin color...

Again, I want what I want...

You know what, Conscience...

I say I a lot...

... ...

Maybe my thoughts should be about other people rather than only thinking about self-indulging wants. I actually have everything needed, yet, like so many other people, I don't think or even care for consequences. The color of someone's skin shouldn't be a factor when selecting someone to be intimate with. It's crazy how the ego takes over everything and makes us so thoughtless. And my ego is greedy.

Conscience, when did the ego become the ruler of humanity? Or was it always superior? Now that I think about it, the ego is at the forefront of most people's lives because we focus on our own desires without even acknowledging the impact our decisions may have on all those around us: our families, friends, neighbors, and coworkers.

Are PEOPLE this selfish? Am I this selfish? Is selfishness the core of HUMANS due to our egotistic desires? Until now, I only saw it as wanting something a little different.

Signed A Cheating Heart

Cheating on your spouse in any contex is horrible, but to desecrate the sanctity of marriage over colorism is top level low-down, dirty and racist. You are telling your mate that they are less than simply because of how they were born. The way God created them. Take that bit of information how you want.

Love who you want to love. The color of a person's skin shouldn't matter. It should be the content of their character. But, if you find someone of a different race attractive, and you are married, (Or even in a commited relationship) make sure you have a clean conscience and is pure of heart while you persue them. Anything else is despicable.

8 SOUL PIRATE

You may as well call yourself the worst thief in the world.

Every time I'm demeaned for how I was created, you steal a piece of my heart. Tearing it apart.

I am who I am. A **HUMAN**. And no matter what anyone told you. That's what I am. I also bleed. What am I to do?

Ripping away my confidence is another way to call you a thief. You want to take away how I feel about myself.

THIEF!!!

How dare you rob me of my happiness. I was quite pleased with how I looked. Until you came along and told me differently.

I believed you when you treated the animals better.

You crept into my head, pilfered my thoughts, and then plagiarized my story.

YOU THIEF YOU!!

Using how I was created to snatch my livelihood while surreptitiously believing as I do.

And while we're on the subject...

Are you appropriating my culture out of admiration, or are you just swiping what you think is cool?

It takes a real asshole to be a thief.

To take something with no intent on giving it back.

To take something you can't give back.

To steal something, that is.

Something like my heart.

My happiness.

My dignity.

My self-esteem.

My Peace.

How I live.

My beliefs.

My culture.

Every time, I'm degraded for how I was created, you may as well call yourself the worst thief in the world.

9 BODY LANGUAGE

It is where the truth dwells. And if you pay attention, it will surely tell the lies a person wears oh so well.

Radiating like a beam of light, it shows the world what is right, no matter how deep you try to keep it hidden from everyone's sight.

Even when we seek to deceive, it's worn right on the sleeve. And again, if you pay close attention, it is so simple to read.

Because it's where the truth dwells. And it will for sure be the tell of the lies a person wears oh so well.

The language is easy to peep. Because it's the body that begins to speak. Every part says something different, from the head down to the feet.

Regardless of what you've been taught, just know that it says a lot. Even when out of your mouth you're screaming, that it's not.

You show me by what you do something that I already knew, that my skin color is causing great distress for some reason to you.

Though I can't fathom why, no matter how hard I try to understand the hatred and fear about a skin type.

Through body language, I get to see what you truly think of me. I became aware of the truth when your words and actions didn't agree.

How do you not get, or better yet, how did you forget, that we're the same person on the inside where the truth is always met.

The heart is the place that has no race or room for evil actions because of the color of a face.

So when you see people who give you a scare, after a quick prayer, remember that your skin is only the suit that God gave you.

STOP WITH THE RACISM

10 What's Appropriate?

Hey, guess what? I'm better!

I'm better than you, you, you, and you.

I don't like the herbs, leaves, and weird healing stuff you use. It don't work, and forget trying to prove to me that it does.

> *But here! Take this elixir. It's made of a bunch of stuff neither one of us can pronounce and cost a lot. Well hey! At least it's in pill form.*

I hate your wardrobe. I know that it's comfortable for you and reflects who you are. However, it does look ridiculous, strange, and cheap, in my opinion. I'm sure others agree.

> *But here! Take these clothes made by the proper people. They fit the trend, and I say that it's the right thing to do. Now we look alike. Oh! Don't worry about the cost or stupid stuff like your culture. You look good.*

I can't stand your taste in food. Even though you say it's natural, part of your heritage, and good for you, it stinks and looks nasty.

> *But here! Take these delicious items made with the finest processed ingredients and on the fastest assembly lines. Don't worry about the plastics and metals. They'll pass in time— maybe not before you. HaHaHa! It's just a joke.*

I detest your name. Even though you say you're proud of it, it's a part of your uniqueness. I don't like it. It's hard to pronounce and too eccentric. It doesn't sound right.

But here! I have this approved list of names. That way, I can prove that you are human, and I'll know how it's pronounced. Never mind merits, knowledge, or expression. I'll be able to understand it better.

I condemn your skin color. It's just not right, not natural, even though everything natural is colorful.

But here! Use these skin-brightening, bleaching, tanning, darkening, or cover-up beauty products to fit the right beauty standard. Never mind the burning, itching, irritated skin... You'll get used to it over time.

Speaking of beauty, I admonish everything about you. You know. Your clothes, shoes, hair, and attitude. Who are you to think you are an individual and created unique?

But here! Take these surgeries. They can shape you and mold you, add and subtract what is needed to make you exactly how you are supposed to be. Don't worry about the fact you can die. It doesn't happen that often... I think.

I snub the place you live. You say you have lived there all your life, and you love it. Well, I'm here to tell you that it looks scary, dangerous, violent, unkept, racist, crowded, and just unpleasant. All those people have one thing in common.

But here! Move into my area where people will not like you, and in order for you to fit in, you will have to change who you are (see above) and don't express yourself in any way. Order must be kept at all times.

I rebuke your belief system. My way is the right way.

But here! Take these books so that you can believe as I believe, even though some of the things I do are against what is said in these books. Also, I do things in vain, but it doesn't matter. Don't think for yourself, and just know that people who look like me are always right.

So, let me remind you! A recap!

What do you mean by you saw me?

Oh! You saw me using healing herbs. Forget that; remember, my elixirs are better.

Don't worry about the chemical effects on your body; doctors say it's best. It's in pill form.

I know you checked me out in the clothes from your culture, but remember, my wardrobe is better. It's made by the right people.

Don't worry that it doesn't fit or isn't unique.

What do you mean you spotted me at your family's restaurant.

Overlook that. My food is better. Ignore the plastics and metals. Oh! And the pesticides. Forgot about that one. Don't worry that I'm not healthy.

My name is better. I know it's not that different from anyone else.

Don't worry that it's common, and your family wants your name to have meaning. And yes, I consider my children's names exotic. That's not of your concern.

My skin color is natural because I made it that way. Ignore the cosmetics and I only bleached, darkened it once.... twice.... I forgot.

It's cool! I visit the doctor next week. I'm always there. Yes, I know you were created that way naturally. So what!

I had plastic surgery two months ago. It's exactly how I wanted it.

Don't worry about me still not being satisfied. Hey! Trends come and go. I really don't care about you being happy about your looks.

Now, as far as where I live, it may take a little work (see above), and you may not be you. But you'll get there.

Don't worry about the shady people (Which are everywhere, by the way), my unhappiness, and the ones that may not like you no matter how much you change. It's a lot to uproot yourself. I know.

And don't forget. I'm the only one that believes the right way. I read a lot of books and listened to a lot of people who have the same skin color as me. And the people I listen to do no wrong. In my eyes, at least.

Throw away what God tells you in your heart and forget that books are written by flawed people. And Oh! That God loves us ALL under creation.

Now that we have all that settled.

Do you understand why I'm better?

S Y M A N T I C S
Sticks and Stones

Sticks and stones may break my bones, but name calling is the driving force behind racism.

What's with all the isms and phobias. Isms are any distinctive practice, system, or philosophy. A phobia is an extreme fear of something. An ism is a way to focus on labeling each other, especially when the goal is to shut others out, and some phobias are used to discriminate. HUMANS are so hyper-focused on identity commonality that we have encased ourselves in boxes of isms and phobias and call them ists. Shutting each other out because of isms and phobias has caused us to be divisive, discriminatory, hostile, and ignorant toward each other while we stifle creation with stereotypes, categorization, and the scramble for power.

Like little children, we call ourselves and each other names. These names come from stereotypes, which come from propaganda, which leads to projection, which fuels jealousy and hatred. When someone is jealous, they become consumed with the desire to possess, control, or destroy. We have become a world filled with egotistical cravings and desires that keep us from putting God First. Including when we allow our ego to do the Lord's work of judgment. Judgment over which religion is the best. Judgment over someone's personal decisions. Judgment over which race is the best.

Xenophobia: Discrimination against people from other countries or anyone deemed "foreign" because of their immigrant or visitor status.

Transphobia: Discrimination against transpeople or gender non-conforming people because of their gender identity.

Islamophobia: Discrimination against anyone practicing or perceived to be a practitioner of Islam because of their religious affiliation.

Atheophobia: Discrimination against anyone who identifies as Atheist or is perceived to be Atheist because of their lack of religious affiliation.

Fatphobia: Discrimination against people with bigger bodies because of their size.

Homophobia/Heterosexism: Discrimination against non-heterosexual people because of their sexuality.

Racism: Prejudice, discrimination or antagonism by an individual, community or institution against a person or people on the basis of their membership in a particular racial or ethnic group, typically one that is a minority or marginalized.

Colorism: Within and between-group discrimination against people of color with darker skin tones and giving preference to people of color with lighter skin tones.

Tokenism: The practice of using people of color in a symbolic gesture to avoid criticism or being called racist.

Anti-Semitism: Discrimination against a Jewish people or people perceived to be Jewish because of their affiliation to Judaism.

Sexism: Prejudice or discrimination based on one's sex or gender. Sexism can affect anyone, but it primarily affects women and girls.

Ableism: Discrimination against people with impaired or limited abilities because of their physical abilities.

Ageism: Discrimination against older populations because of their age and perceived competence or capabilities.

Classism: Discrimination against people of lower class because of their economic status.

Elitism: Discrimination against people believed to be "less than" in terms of education, money, job status/position, etc.

Anarchism: Doctrine that all governments should be abolished.

Atheism: Belief that there is no God.

Capitalism: Doctrine that private ownership and free markets should govern economies.

Communism: Theory of a classless society in which individuals cannot own property.

Conservatism: Belief in maintaining political and social traditions.

Deism: Belief in God but rejection of religion.

Egalitarianism: Belief that humans ought to be equal in rights and privileges.

Existentialism: Doctrine of individual human responsibility in an unfathomable universe.

Fascism: A far-right form of government in which most of the country's power is held by one ruler or a small group, under a single party. Fascist governments are usually totalitarian and authoritarian one-party states.

Hedonism: Belief that pleasure is the highest good.

Humanitarianism: Doctrine that the highest moral obligation is to improve human welfare.

Idealism: Belief that our experiences of the world consist of ideas.

Liberalism: Doctrine of social change and tolerance.

Libertarianism: Doctrine that personal liberty is the highest value.

Materialism: Belief that matter is the only extant substance.

Messianism: Belief in a single messiah or savior.

Monotheism: Belief in only one God.

Naturalism: Belief that the world can be explained in terms of natural forces.

Pansexualism: Theory that all thought is derived from sexual instinct.

Philanthropism: The practice of giving time, talent, or money to help others,

Polytheism: Belief in multiple deities.

Pragmatism: Emphasizing the practical value of philosophy.

Quietism: Doctrine of enlightenment through mental tranquility.

Republicanism: Belief that a republic is the best form of government.

Romanticism: Belief in sentimental feeling in artistic expression.

Sexism: Belief in systematic inequalities between the sexes.

Skepticism: Doctrine that true knowledge is always uncertain.

Socialism: Doctrine of centralized state control of wealth and property.

Spiritualism: Belief that nothing is real except the soul or spirit.

Stoicism: Belief in indifference to pleasure or pain.

Zionism: International effort working in the beginning for a Jewish homeland and later for the support of Israel.

https://engineering.osu.edu/quick-guide-isms-and-phobias

When I found out how many ways we use labels to separate ourselves just with isms alone, I was blown away. I chose the ones we throw at each other the most currently in 2024. There are over 200 different isms and phobias we box ourselves in, causing everyone in the world to be full of ists.

W E H A D 1 J O B !
The Final Chapter: A Rant!

We've been told over and over again. Regardless of how you believe, what you have, or how you look, as humans, we have only one job.

Admittedly, I don't know the ins and outs of most religions, but from what I can gather, the messages are all the same. Love seems to be the primary theme across every major belief system. It is my personal belief that The Creator has embodied the HUMAN form many times and approaches each of us in the way that is most comfortable. Also, we choose to deny the omnipotence and place Him in a personal religious box suitable for the ego.

Nowhere in any of the religious texts practiced today (as far as I have noticed) is the "Hate them because of the color of their skin" section. Well, not according to these brief ideals of love, based on the most practiced religions in 2024. You begin to find the hate sentiment once you get past the original purpose for the religion, and HUMANS begin to make up their own version of a belief.

HINDUISM. In Hinduism, there are considered to be five stages of love: Atma Prema, Bhakti, Maitri, Shringara, and Kama. Atma Prema is a form of self love that is cultivated through loving others. The more one pours love out the more love returns to them (this is based on the ideal that all are one.) Bhakti is a love that extends to all of creation and further connects to the love of God. Maitri is considered to be a compassionate love that exists through kindness for all. Shringara is a romantic love, specifically the intimacy found between romantic partners. Finally, Kama is a love stirred by attraction and sexual desire.

BUDDHISM. Buddhism has four elements of what is considered to be true love. Maitri, Karuna, Mudita, and Upeksha. Just like in Hinduism, Maitri is a form of love born through acts of kindness. Karuna is a compassionate love that focuses on the ability to understand one another and to be able to aid/help/assist someone else. Mudita is simply known to be joy (the absence of joy in love is not believed to be true love). The fourth and final element is Upeksha which is inclusiveness. This love is one of acceptance and non-discrimination.

JUDAISM. In Judaism, the fundamental forms of love are the love of God, neighbor and strangers. One of the core commandments of Judaism is "Love your neighbor as yourself." This commandment stands at the center of the central book in the Torah.

CHRISTIANITY. The Christian Bible speaks directly of two different forms of love (although more may be interpreted): Philia and Agape. Philia is described as brotherly love. It is a love that is found between neighbors, friends, family, and demonstrated to strangers. Agape is a divine love. It is considered to be an unconditional, and selfless love from God to mankind. Within Christianity there is a large emphasis on this spiritual love.

> *"A new command I give you: Love one another. As I have loved you, so you must love one another. By this everyone will know that you are my disciples, if you love one another." New International Version John 13:34-35*

ISLAM. Islamic sacred texts describe two major forms of love, one being divine love and the other human love. Divine love is the love of God as well as the love people hold for God. Through this love comes human love, which is considered to be a comprehensive love to all creations of God, from insects to humans, with particular emphasis between humans such as strangers, friends, family, and romantic partners.

Core Teachings of the Prophet Muhammad Peace be Upon Him

Classical scholars of Islam have condensed the teachings of Prophet Muhammad into a few statements. These comprehensive statements touch every aspect of our lives. Some of them are:

1) Actions are judged by the intention behind them.

2) God is Pure and does not accept anything unless it is pure and God has commanded the faithful with what He commanded the prophets.

3) Part of a person's good observance of Islam is to leave aside what does not concern him.

4) A person cannot be a complete believer unless he loves for his brother what he loves for himself.

5) One should not harm himself or others.

6) Don't let your focus in this life be to amass worldly gain and God will love you. Don't be concerned with what people have, and they will love you. *https://www.lincolncentralmosque. org.uk/core-teachings-of-the-prophet-muhammad-peace-be-upon-him/*

SIKHISM. In Sikhism, Pyare means love for the Lord and His creation. This is one of five virtues that is vigorously promoted by the Sikh Gurus. The other four qualities are: Truth (Sat), Contentment (Santokh), Compassion (Daya) and Humility (Nimrata). These five qualities are essential to Sikhs and their religious obligations. It is their belief that when your mind is full of love, you can accept anyone as God's creation.

Taken from https://faithcounts.com/love-in-every-religion/

The Creator has been and always will be about love. Throughout the history of humanity's existence, the commandment of love has been the one thing that is constantly demanded of us. We have one job. It seems like a simple and logical task; however, the vinegar to the sweetness of love has become too overpowering. We are choosing as a collective to tear each other apart and everything we are to be rulers of, because of who we are. Because of how we feel. Because of how we choose to worship. Because of the color of our skin. Because of the ego. None are perfect because Assholes Come In All Colors so.....

When did the ego become the main religion of mankind?

Or was it always the case?

LOVE EACH OTHER BEFORE THERE'S NOTHING ELSE TO LOVE.

RACISM FASCISM RUSCISM

VIOLENCE Terrorism

PROPAGANDA Hate AGGRESSION

WAR

www.ingramcontent.com/pod-product-compliance
Lightning Source LLC
Chambersburg PA
CBHW041218270326
41931CB00001B/27